BIG HOUSE RECIPES

*Delicious food
for outdoor eating*

*Compiled by
Simon Haseltine*

SALMON

Index

Barbecued Fish with a Mediterranean
 Sauce 7
Barbecued Fruit 35
Barbecued Sweet Potato Salad 24
Barbecued Vegetable Salad 13
Barbecue Sauce 22
Beach Loaf 42
Beach Party Dips and Nibbles 40
Bonfire Night Soup 29
Boozy Strawberries in Red Wine 32
Camp Fire Dampers 38
Cheeseburgers 21
Chorizo Stew 3
Christmas Day Walk Mincemeat Slice 37
Crab Chowder 30
Crab Roll 43
Cullen Skink 27
Devilled Whitebait with Homemade
 Tartare Sauce 15

First Jersey Royal Potato Kebabs 26
Fish Cakes 8
Fish Curry 19
Fish Kebabs with Basil Sauce 6
Fruity Milk Smoothies 46
Fruity Pimms Lollies 45
Ginger Beer 47
Homemade Seaside Coleslaw 23
Hot Dogs with a Spicy Relish 11
Kedgeree 10
Mediterranean Mussels 16
Paella 18
Poached Cod with Parsley Sauce 5
Seaside Fish Stew 14
Smoked Salmon Pate 31
Toffee Apples 39
Traditional Knickerbocker Glory 34

Printed and Published by J. Salmon Ltd., Sevenoaks, England © Copyright

Title page photograph: ALAMY

Chorizo Stew

A tasty seaside supper...

6 spring onions (chopped)	350g chorizo sausage (chopped)
Oil (from frying)	100g soft dried apricots (chopped)
400g bulgar wheat	2 x 400g cans chickpeas (drained)
Good pinch dried mixed herbs	1 x 400g can ratatouille
800ml chicken stock	1 x 400g chopped tomatoes
2 bay leaves	Tabasco sauce (to taste)

Small bunch coriander (chopped)

Sauté the spring onion in a little oil for a minute or so to soften, then add the bulgar wheat and fry for a further 2 minutes. Stir in the herbs and stock , add the bay leaves, bring to the boil and then simmer with a lid on for 15 minutes, or until the wheat is cooked. In a second pan, add the chorizo to a little oil and sauté for 5 minutes. Stir in the apricots, chickpeas, ratatouille and tomatoes, together with a splash of Tabasco sauce and simmer for 10 minutes. Remove the bay leaves and serve the stew on a bed of the bulgar wheat with the chopped coriander sprinkled over the top and some crusty bread on the side. Serves 4.

Poached Cod with Parsley Sauce

A classic lunchtime dish for your beach house...

4 cod fillets	1 bay leaf
450ml milk	Large knob butter
450ml fish stock	1 tablespoon plain flour
1 tsp mixed herbs	Bunch parsley (chopped)
1 lemon (juice only)	

Add the fish fillets, milk, fish stock, mixed herbs and bay leaf to a large sauté pan and simmer gently for 5 minutes or until the fish is cooked through. Remove the fish and keep warm; discard the bay leaf. In a separate pan, melt the butter and mix in the flour, stirring over a low heat for a few minutes. Now gradually add the poaching liquid and parsley and bring back to the boil then simmer for a minute or two until the sauce thickens. Remove from the heat, add the lemon juice and pour over the fish. Serve with some fresh summer peas and new potatoes. Serves 4.

Fish Kebabs with Basil Sauce

A fishy addition to your beach barbecue, which you can prepare at home and take with you...

½ red, ½ yellow and ½ green pepper
4 fish fillets
(use a combination of cod, smoked haddock and salmon – cut into bite size pieces)
1 lemon (juice only)   Glug olive oil   Seasoning (to taste)
Basil Sauce:
1 tbsp white wine vinegar   1 clove garlic (minced)
Bunch basil leaves (chopped finely)   3 tbsp olive oil
3 tbsp double cream   1 egg yolk (beaten)

Prepare the peppers by deseeding and cutting into small bite size pieces and place in a basin. Add the fish, lemon juice, a good glug of olive oil and seasoning and marinate for 30 minutes. To make the basil sauce, add the oil, vinegar, garlic, basil and cream to a small saucepan and heat gently for a few minutes, stirring all the time. Add the egg yolk and a little seasoning and return to the hob. Simmer very gently for a few more minutes, stirring all the time, until the sauce thickens. Remove from the heat and pour the sauce into a thermos flask to keep warm. Down on the beach, place the marinated fish and peppers onto skewers and grill over the barbecue or camp fire embers for around 5 minutes, turning every minute or so. Serve with the warm basil sauce, a crispy salad and chunky bread. Serves 4.

Barbecued Fish with a Mediterranean Sauce

A recipe which you can prepare at home and take to the beach barbecue...

4 fish fillets (use cod or salmon)   1 lemon (juice only)
Olive oil   Seasoning

Mediterranean Sauce:

2 Spanish onions (chopped)   1 tbsp tomato puree
4 cloves garlic   Pinch dried Provence herbs
Olive oil   Bunch basil leaves (chopped)
2 tins of chopped tomatoes   Seasoning (to taste)

Marinade the fish with the olive oil and lemon juice and season lightly. To make the sauce, sauté the onions and garlic in a pan with a little oil for 5 minutes until softened. Add the tinned tomatoes, tomato puree, mixed herbs, basil leaves and seasoning and simmer for 20 minutes or so, stirring occasionally. Pour the sauce into a thermos flask and take to the beach with the marinated fish. Over the BBQ, gently grill the fish fillets for 5 minutes until the fish is cooked through. Serve with the warm Mediterranean sauce and a sliced tomato and mozzarella salad, drizzled with olive oil. Serves 4.

Fish Cakes

Nothing beats homemade fish cakes for taste...

Around 700g cooked mashed potato with butter
Around 500g cooked fish flaked (cod, smoked haddock, salmon all work well)
2 tbsp capers (chopped)   Small bunch chives (cut small)
Small bunch parsley (chopped)   Seasoning (to taste)
2 eggs (beaten)   125g breadcrumbs   Oil

In a large bowl, combine the mashed potato, cooked fish flakes, capers, chives and parsley and mix well with a fork. Shape the fish mixture into 8 equally sized balls, then flatten to form fish cakes. Cover and place in the fridge to chill for a few hours. When ready to cook, place the beaten egg into a shallow dish and the breadcrumbs on a plate. Dip each fishcake into the egg, then cover with breadcrumbs and fry in some hot oil for 5 minutes each side until they are cooked through and golden brown. Serve with a good dollop of tomato ketchup and a green salad.   Makes 8 fishcakes.

Beach hut at Mersea Island, Essex

Kedgeree

Breakfast on the beach...

6 spring onions (chopped)   1 tbsp curry powder
300g basmati rice   100g peas (a small cup full)
675ml chicken stock   500g smoked haddock or cod
Milk (for poaching)
2 eggs (hardboiled – shelled and quartered)
Small bunch coriander (shredded)
1 lemon (quartered)

Sauté the spring onions in a large pan for 5 minutes until softened, then add the curry powder and cook through for a further 2 minutes, stirring all the time. Add the rice, peas and stock and simmer for 15 minutes or until the rice is cooked through. Meanwhile, poach the haddock or cod in a little milk for 5 minutes until cooked. Remove from the pan and flake into bite size chunks (whilst checking for bones). When the rice is cooked, mix with the fish and eggs and heat through for a further 2 minutes. Scatter with coriander and serve with a wedge of lemon. Serves 4.

Hot Dogs with a Spicy Relish

A quick and simple recipe with a delicious spicy relish...

1 can of jumbo hot dogs (6 in a can)   6 bridge rolls
American mustard   Watercress (to serve)
Relish:
2 Spanish onions (thinly sliced)
Oil   2 cloves garlic (minced)
1 tsp cumin seeds   1 tsp mustard seeds
1 red chilli (sliced)   2 tbsp light muscovado sugar
30ml red wine vinegar

At home, sauté the onions in a little oil for around 10 minutes until they start to turn brown. Stir in the garlic, cumin, mustard seeds and chilli and fry for a further minute. Add the sugar and vinegar and gently simmer for 5 minutes or until the liquid reduces to a jam like consistency. Remove the relish to a serving dish and allow to cool. In the beach hut, heat the sausages in a pan on your picnic stove until hot. To serve, squirt some American mustard along the bottom of each bridge roll, top with a hot dog, a dollop of relish and some fiery watercress. Serves 6.

Barbecued Vegetable Salad

A delicious vegetarian option for the barbecue...

2 beef tomatoes   1 green pepper
1 red pepper   2 aubergines
1 Spanish onion (sliced)
30ml balsamic vinegar
Small bunch fresh herbs
(a combination of dill, coriander and parsley works best)
Olive oil   1 lemon (juice only)   Watercress (to serve)

Place the beef tomatoes, peppers and aubergines on the barbecue for 30 minutes, turning every 10 minutes, until charred, softened and cooked through. Remove from the heat and allow to cool for 15 minutes, then peel away the skins; core and deseed the peppers then roughly chop all the vegetables into bite size pieces and place in a bowl. Add onions, balsamic vinegar, chopped herbs, a drizzle of olive oil and the lemon juice. Mix. Top with a bunch of watercress and serve with a slice of crusty bread. Serves 6.

Seaside Fish Stew

A delicious stew using local seasonal produce...

2 onions (sliced)   500g potato (cubed)   Oil
2 garlic cloves (chopped)   1 tsp paprika   Pinch cayenne pepper(to taste)
1 lemon (juice)   1 can chopped tomatoes
1 fish stock cube (dissolved in half a can of hot water)
Seasoning (to taste)
500g fish fillets (any combination – skin removed, cut into bite size chunks)
200g raw peeled king prawn   1 can chickpeas (drained)
Bunch parsley (chopped)   Lemon zest   Olive oil

Sauté onions and potatoes in a little oil for 5 minutes until the onion has softened. Add the garlic and spices, then cook for a further 2 minutes. Next, add the lemon juice, chopped tomatoes and the fish stock, season to taste and simmer for 20 minutes until the potatoes are just cooked. Stir through the fish, prawns and chickpeas, reduce the heat and simmer with the lid on for 10 minutes, stirring gently half way through. To serve: scatter with parsley, add the lemon zest and a drizzle of olive oil. Serves 4.

Devilled Whitebait with Homemade Tartare Sauce

A wonderful supper dish everyone can cook for themselves...

Tartare Sauce:
300g mayonnaise   1 large red onion (finely chopped)
60g capers (sliced)   Small bunch parsley (chopped)
Small bunch tarragon (chopped)   Small bunch chervil (chopped)
Seasoning (to taste)

Fish:
200g plain flour   1 tbsp smoked paprika   Pinch cayenne pepper
2 tsp mustard powder   Seasoning (to taste)
500g whitebait   Oil (for frying)   1 lemon (quartered)

To make the tartare sauce, dollop the mayonnaise into a bowl, then add the remaining ingredients until well mixed. Store in the fridge until required. Next, mix the flour, paprika, cayenne pepper, mustard powder and a pinch of salt, then coat the whitebait until well covered. Fry in a large sauté pan in the hot oil for a few minutes until golden brown, turning once. Drain on some kitchen paper and serve warm with a dollop of your homemade tartare sauce and a quarter of lemon. Serves 4.

Mediterranean Mussels

Bring a taste of the warm Mediterranean to your very own seaside…

Olive oil
250g chorizo (sliced)
1 Spanish onion (chopped)
2 garlic cloves (chopped)
150ml red wine

2 bay leaves
2 tins chopped tomatoes
1 tsp smoked paprika
1.5 kg mussels (cleaned)
Bunch coriander (chopped)

In a large sauté pan, add some olive oil and fry the chorizo for a few minutes, then add the onions and garlic and continue cooking for a further 5 minutes or until the onions have softened. Add the red wine, and cook off for a minute or so. Next, add the bay leaves, chopped tomatoes, smoked paprika and boil for 2 minutes. Stir in the mussels, then cover and steam for 2 minutes until the mussels open (discard any that do not open). Remove the bay leaves and add the coriander. Serve in bowls with a chunk of crusty bread to mop up all the juices.

Shellfish meal at low tide

Paella

The perfect supper dish for a beach party...

Olive oil   100g chorizo sausage (sliced)
2 red onions (chopped)   2 garlic cloves (chopped)
1 tsp smoked paprika   Pinch dried mixed herbs
300g paella rice   Glug white wine
1 can chopped tomatoes   900ml chicken stock   Seasoning
400g Seafood mix
(shop bought mixture of cod and salmon fish chunks, prawns, squid etc)
Bunch parsley (chopped)   2 lemons (1 for juice, 1 quartered)

In a large sauté pan, heat a little oil and fry the chorizo for 2 minutes before adding the onion and garlic, then fry for a further 5 minutes until the onion has softened. Add the paprika, herbs and rice, stir to coat the rice, then add a glug of white wine. Cook off for a minute or so, then add the tomatoes and stock. Season and simmer for 15 minutes until the rice is tender, stirring a few times. Stir in the prepared seafood, cover and simmer for 5 minutes or until cooked through. Scatter with parsley and add the lemon juice. Serve with the lemon quarters. Serves 4.

Fish Curry

A fiery curry to accompany any beach hut supper party...

2 red onions (sliced)   Oil (for frying)
4 garlic cloves (chopped)   2 teaspoons ginger (grated)
1 tbsp madras curry powder
1 red chilli (seeds removed and chopped)
300ml passata   100ml coconut milk
Sea salt (for seasoning)
500g white fish fillets (bite size pieces)
1 lemon (juice)
Bunch coriander leaves (chopped)
4 portions rice (to serve)

In a large sauté pan, sauté the onion in the oil for 5 minutes until softened. Next, add the garlic, ginger, curry powder, chilli and sauté for 2 further minutes. Add the passata, coconut milk and a pinch of sea salt; stir well and simmer for 10 minutes. Add the fish to the sauce and simmer for 5 minutes or until the fish is cooked through. Squeeze in the lemon juice and scatter with the coriander. Serve with rice. Serves 4.

Cheeseburgers

Beach food and not just for the kids...

500g minced beef
150g breadcrumbs
Pinch mixed herbs
100g mature cheddar (grated)
Splash Worcestershire sauce
Parsley

1 egg (beaten)
Salt and pepper (to season)
6 burger buns
2 beef tomatoes (sliced)
1 red onion (sliced into rings)
Tomato sauce

Place the mince in a bowl, then add the breadcrumbs, herbs, cheese, Worcestershire sauce, parsley, egg and a little seasoning. Mix with your hands until well combined, then shape into 6 burgers and chill in the fridge for a few hours. Place the burgers on the barbecue and cook for around 8 minutes each side or until cooked through. Serve in a bun topped with sliced tomato and onions, together with a dollop of tomato sauce. Serves 6.

Barbecue Sauce

Fancy making this quick barbecue sauce for your beach party...

400g tomato ketchup
4 tbsp Worcestershire sauce
3 tsp wholegrain mustard
½ tsp smoked paprika

Pinch dried mixed herbs
Dash Tabasco sauce
1 lemon (juice)
Seasoning (to taste)

In a saucepan, stir together the tomato ketchup, Worcestershire sauce, mustard, paprika, herbs, tabasco and lemon juice. Simmer for 2 minutes, then remove from the heat and season to taste. Serve as a barbecue sauce or use as a marinade for chicken or spare ribs. Serves 6.

Homemade Seaside Coleslaw

What better accompaniment to a picnic or barbecue on the beach...

1 white cabbage (finely shredded)
2 Spanish onions (finely sliced)
8 small carrots (grated)
10 tbsp mayonnaise
1 lemon (juice only)
2 tsp ready-made mustard (Dijon or English)
Seasoning (to taste)

Prepare the vegetables as shown above and place in a large bowl. In a small bowl, add the mayonnaise, lemon juice and mustard, season to taste and stir well. Add to the vegetables and mix until they are evenly coated. Chill in the fridge for a few hours before serving with a seaside picnic or barbecue.

For a variation, add 1 tbsp of toasted cumin seeds instead of the mustard for an extra bite. Serves 8.

Barbecued Sweet Potato Salad

Here's a salad dish you can make on the beach to impress your friends...

4 sweet potatoes   4 sprigs thyme
Olive oil   Salt (to season)
1 Spanish onion (sliced)
1 beef tomato (chopped)
1 chilli pepper (diced)
Small bunch mint (chopped)
Small bunch parsley (chopped)
Small bunch coriander (chopped)
1 lime (juice only)

Heat the barbecue coals until they are glowing embers. Cut the sweet potatoes in half lengthways and sandwich the thyme sprig, a splash of olive oil and a dash of salt between the 2 halves. Double wrap each sweet potato in foil and bake in the embers for around 30 minutes until cooked through (check with a skewer). Next, unwrap the foil and remove the thyme sprig. Holding the hot potato in a cloth, peel away the skin and chop into bitesize chunks. In a bowl, gently toss together the sweet potato chunks, onion, tomato, chilli and herbs. Drizzle with lime juice and serve warm with barbecued chicken. Serves 6.

'Anyone for tea?' – Cornish Beach house

First Jersey Royal Potato Kebabs

A delicious celebration for the first Jersey Royal Potatoes…

1 kg Jersey Royal Potatoes
1 garlic clove (crushed)
Bunch chives (finely chopped)

75g butter (softened)
Salt and black pepper(to taste)
Olive oil

Place the potatoes in a pan and simmer for around 15 minutes until they are just cooked through. Drain and set aside. Mix together the garlic, chives and butter, then season to taste. On the beach barbecue, thread the cooked potatoes on skewers, brush with a little oil and "roast" over the embers for 10 minutes, turning until golden brown. Smother with the garlic and chive butter (which you can soften by keeping near the barbecue embers) and enjoy with a seasonal salad. Serves 6.

Cullen Skink

A classic recipe for this traditional Scottish fish soup...

100ml milk	1 onion (chopped)
400ml vegetable stock	1 large potato (chopped)
2 smoked haddock fillets	Small bunch parsley (chopped)
Large knob butter	30ml double cream

Heat the milk and 200ml of the vegetable stock until just simmering. Add the smoked haddock and simmer for around 5 minutes until cooked. Remove from the heat, place the fish on a plate and using a fork separate into small chunks, removing any skin or bones. Reserve the poaching liquid. Meanwhile, in a second pan, melt the butter and then sauté the onion for 5 minutes until softened. Add the potato and remaining stock, then simmer for 20 minutes or until the potato has cooked. Next, add the poaching liquid and blend until smooth. Return to the saucepan, add the smoked haddock and parsley and simmer for a few minutes to heat through. Stir through the double cream and serve with crusty rolls. Serves 4.

Bonfire Night Soup

Hot soup in a mug to warm your hands and tummy on a chilly bonfire night on the beach...

3 parsnips (scraped and diced)
2 carrots (scraped and diced)
3 tbsp maple syrup   Olive oil   1 large onion (chopped)
1 large Bramley apple (peeled and diced)
500ml vegetable stock   100ml cider
30ml double cream

Preheat the oven to 180C/350F/gas 4. Cover the parsnips and carrots with the maple syrup and a little olive oil. Place on a baking tray and roast in the oven for 30 minutes until golden. Add a glug of oil to a sauté pan and fry the onion for 5 minutes until softened. Add the apples, roasted parsnips and carrots, vegetable stock and cider, and simmer for 20 minutes until the apples are cooked through. Remove from the heat and allow to cool slightly. Blend until smooth, then add the cream and reheat to serve. Serves 4.

Crab Chowder

A hearty soup for a beach luncheon…

Knob butter   1 Spanish onion (diced)
Small packet pancetta cubes (around 1 cup full)
4 sticks celery (sliced)   2 potatoes (cut into small cubes)
2 large cans sweetcorn   3 tbsp plain flour
1 tsp mustard powder   300ml white wine
Small tub single cream   450ml milk
200g crab meat (cooked)
1 lemon (juice only)
Small bunch parsley (chopped)

In a large pan, melt the butter and sauté the onion, pancetta cubes and celery for 5 minutes or until the onion has softened. Add the potatoes and sweet corn kernels, stir and sauté for a further 5 minutes. Next, stir in the flour and mustard powder and cook for a minute or so, then add the wine, cream and milk. Bring to the boil and simmer for 20 minutes or until the potato has cooked through. Remove from the heat and add the crab meat. Serve in individual soup bowls with a little lemon juice and a sprinkling of parsley leaves. Serves 4.

Smoked Salmon Pate

Serve on toast as a tasty starter or nibbles at any beach party...

300g smoked salmon fillets (cooked)   150g cream cheese
1 lemon (juice only)   3 tsp horseradish sauce
Seasoning(to taste)

Skin and flake the cooked fish, add the lemon juice, cream cheese and horseradish sauce. Season to taste and mash to a course texture with a fork. Spoon into a small serving dish, cover with cling film. Press down with some food tins and chill for a few hours. Serve on cold crispy toast with a salad garnish. Serves 4.

Boozy Strawberries in Red Wine

An adult's version of strawberries and cream...

1 kg strawberries (hulled – leave 6 unhulled)
4 tablespoons caster sugar
1 bottle sweet red wine
300ml tub double cream
1 tablespoon icing sugar

Place the hulled strawberries in a large bowl and dredge with the caster sugar, then pour over enough of the wine to just cover the strawberries. Leave in the fridge for an hour or so to chill. Meanwhile, whip the cream with the icing sugar to form soft peaks. Serve the strawberries and wine in individual sundae glasses, topped with a dollop of cream and a whole strawberry on top. Serves 6.

Deckchairs on Swanage Beach, Dorset

Traditional Knickerbocker Glory

Surely, the ultimate seaside desert…

1 pint strawberry jelly (made up but not set)
2 tins mixed fruit salad (drained)
Tub vanilla ice cream
300ml double cream (whipped)
Bottle strawberry sauce
4 Glacé cherries
Tub hundreds and thousands to decorate

Pour the strawberry jelly equally into 4 tall sundae glasses and allow to set. Next, add a layer of the fruit salad from one of the tins, followed by a dollop of ice cream. Now, add the second tin of fruit salad and another dollop of ice cream. Top with the whipped cream and a large squirt of strawberry sauce. Pop a glacé cherry on the top, sprinkle with the hundreds and thousands and serve immediately, with a long spoon. Serves 4.

Barbecued Fruit

A delicious pudding to cook on the dying embers of the barbecue...

200g caster sugar plus a little extra
2 oranges (juice)   250g mascarpone cheese
150ml coconut cream   Vanilla essence
3 tbsp icing sugar
Black pepper (to taste)
6 thick slices pineapple (peeled)
6 mango halves   6 peach halves

In a heavy based saucepan, melt the caster sugar over a low heat until amber in colour. Remove from the heat and add the orange juice, return to the heat and stir for a few more minutes, then set aside to cool. In a bowl, beat the mascarpone, coconut cream, a drop of vanilla essence and the icing sugar until smooth. Sprinkle a little of the extra caster sugar and a grind of black pepper over the cut side of each fruit piece, then barbecue over the embers for around 5 minutes or until lightly charred. Arrange the fruit pieces on a serving plate and drizzle over the orange syrup. Top with a dollop of the mascarpone cream. Serves 6.

Christmas Day Walk Mincemeat Slices

Perfect for a cold and frosty Christmas morning stroll along the beach...

225g wholemeal flour   2 tsp baking powder
75g unsalted butter (softened) + some for greasing
75g demerara sugar   1 egg (beaten)
115g mincemeat (from a jar)   4 tbsp milk
½ cup porridge oats
demerara sugar (to sprinkle)

Preheat the oven to 200C/400F/Gas 6. Line the base of an 11″ x 7″ shallow baking tin and butter the sides. Sift the flour and baking powder into a bowl; add the softened butter and mix with your fingers until the mixture resembles bread crumbs. Add the demerara sugar, egg and mincemeat and mix with enough of the milk to form a soft dough. Spread evenly over the prepared baking tray and sprinkle with porridge oats and demerara sugar. Bake in the oven for 20 minutes until firm and golden. Remove from the oven and allow to cool in the baking tray before cutting into rectangle slices. Makes 12 bars.

Beachside houses at Sidmouth, East Devon

Camp Fire Dampers

Sweet or savoury – for a beach camp fire...

Sweet:	Savoury:
500g self-raising flour	500g self-raising flour
Pinch salt	Pinch salt
100g caster sugar	100g Cheddar cheese (grated)
200ml water	200ml water
Jar strawberry jam	Jar of pickles

You will need some green sticks (willow or hazel works best), around 60cm long. In a large bowl: Sweet- mix the flour, salt, sugar and water; Savoury – mix the flour, salt, cheese and water until a stiff dough is formed. Divide into small pieces of dough and roll between your hands into a long thin sausage shapes. Wrap each sausage of dough around a stick and bake over the embers of the camp fire for around 10 minutes until cooked (tap with finger for a hollow sound). Serve dipped in either the strawberry jam (sweet) or pickles (savoury). Serves 8.

Toffee Apples

Quintessentially, the traditional British seaside treat...

6 crisp green eating apples   1 tsp vinegar
300g golden caster sugar   3 tbsp golden syrup
6 wooden skewers

Place the apples in a large bowl and cover with boiling water for a minute or so. Remove, pat dry and insert a wooden skewer in the stalk end of each apple. Place the apples on a tray covered with grease proof paper. Pour the sugar into a heavy based saucepan and heat until dissolved, then stir in the vinegar and syrup. Bring back to the boil and, using a sugar thermometer, heat to 150c. Reduce heat to keep the toffee mixture hot and carefully dip each apple into the mixture, twisting until thoroughly coated. Place the toffee apples back on the grease proof paper to harden. Serves 6.

Beach Party Dips and Nibbles

A healthy addition to your beach picnic...

1 red pepper   1 green pepper
4 baby carrots   6 celery sticks
½ cucumber   2 small courgettes
Bunch spring onions   Selection breadsticks
Selection of dips (taramasalata, houmous, yoghurt and chive etc)

Prepare the vegetables: for the peppers, cut in half and remove the pith and seeds, then cut into strips; scrub the carrots, top and tail, then slice into sticks; wash the celery and slice each stick in half lengthways; cut the cucumber and courgettes into segments and then slice into sticks; trim the spring onions but leave whole. Chill the vegetables for a few hours, then serve alongside the breadsticks and pots of dips. Serves 6.

'Ready for the cook'

Beach Loaf

A great idea for a hearty picnic lunch...

1 red pepper (quartered)   1 green pepper (quartered)   2 courgettes (sliced)
Tub mushrooms (sliced)   1 aubergine (sliced)   Olive oil   Splash red wine vinegar
2 garlic cloves (crushed)   Bunch basil leaves   Large (800g) crusty loaf
300g mozzarella (sliced)   Seasoning   4 beef tomatoes (sliced)

Preheat the grill. Place the prepared vegetables (not the tomatoes) into a large bowl and drizzle with olive oil. Grill a batch of vegetables for around 5 minutes each side until tender and just golden. Set aside and repeat until all the vegetables are cooked. Meanwhile, mix a splash of olive oil with the vinegar and garlic and toss through the cooked vegetables with half the basil leaves. Leave to marinade for 2 hours or so. Next, cut the top third off the loaf and scoop out the bread from both the base and lid, leaving a thick edge. Drain and slice the mozzarella and drain the marinading vegetables; pat dry with kitchen towel. Place the vegetables and mozzarella into the bread cavity in layers, together with a sprinkling of the remaining basil leaves. Season the sliced tomatoes and carefully place them into the lid, then place the lid back onto the filled loaf. Wrap the loaf tightly with cling film and place a small tray on top. Weigh down with weights or food tins for 2 hours in a cool place. Unwrap and slice into chunks to serve cold with a fresh salad. Serves 8.

Crab Roll

A taste of the sea – in a roll...

400g white crab meat	400g brown crab meat
1 lime (juice and zest)	Lemon zest
Bunch parsley (chopped)	4 large rolls (baps)
2 tbsp mayonnaise	50g butter (softened)
Salt (to taste)	Little gem lettuce
Pinch cayenne pepper	4 wallys (pickled gherkins) (sliced)
2 beef tomatoes (sliced)	

First, dress the white crab meat with half the lime juice, a pinch of finely grated lime zest, the parsley and the mayonnaise, together with a pinch salt and a little cayenne pepper. Next, dress the brown crab meat with the remaining half of the lime juice, lemon zest and a pinch of salt. Cut the rolls in half and spread with butter, then toast under the grill for a few minutes until just golden brown. Place on a plate and spread each roll with the dressed brown crab meat, then add a layer of lettuce leaves, before topping with the dressed white crab meat. Layer the sliced wallys and tomato on the top, then close the lid and serve. Serves 4.

Fruity Pimms Lollies

An adult's version of a cooling lolly...

Makes 10 (using large lolly moulds)
300ml Pimms
850ml lemonade
10 strawberries (hulled and chopped)
Chunk cucumber (10 small dices)
1 orange (zest only)
Small bunch mint leaves (chopped)
10 lolly sticks

In a large jug, mix together the Pimms and lemonade. Equally divide the strawberry and cucumber pieces into each lolly mould, together with a pinch of orange zest and a couple of chopped mint leaves. Fill the moulds with the Pimms mixture, insert a lolly stick and freeze for 3 hours until firm.

Fruity Milk Smoothies

There is always an abundance of fruit in the summertime,
so here is a healthy and refreshing drink to make...

500g mixture of strawberries, raspberries and blueberries
4 bananas
750ml milk
300ml natural yogurt
Sprigs mint (to decorate)

Prepare the fruit by hulling and halving the strawberries, as well as peeling and chopping the bananas. Place all the ingredients into a food processor and blend until smooth. Serve cold in glasses with a sprig of mint to decorate. Serves 6.

Ginger Beer

Surely the best pop for a beach party...

Makes 5 ltrs
4.5 ltrs cold water (1.5 ltrs and 3 ltrs)
75g fresh ginger (grated)
2 lemons (sliced)
500g golden caster sugar
1 tsp cream of tartar
Sachet yeast

Place 1.5 ltrs of the water into a large stockpot, together with the grated ginger, sliced lemons, sugar and cream of tartar. Heat gently, stirring all the time, until the sugar has dissolved, then bring to the boil and remove from the heat. Next, add the remaining 3 ltrs of cold water and stir in the yeast. Cover and leave overnight in a cool room. The following morning, strain the ginger beer into a jug and pour into pressure proof (plastic pop) bottles, leaving a 5cm gap at the neck. Screw the lids on tightly and store in a cool place, releasing the gas every few hours by slightly unscrewing the lids. The ginger beer will be ready after 48 hours. Serve chilled.

METRIC CONVERSIONS

The weights, measures and oven temperatures used in the preceding recipes can be easily converted to their metric equivalents. The conversions listed below are only approximate, having been rounded up or down as may be appropriate.

Weights

Avoirdupois	Metric
1 oz.	just under 30 grams
4 oz. (¼ lb.)	app. 115 grams
8 oz. (½ lb.)	app. 230 grams
1 lb.	454 grams

Liquid Measures

Imperial	Metric
1 tablespoon (liquid only)	20 millilitres
1 fl. oz.	app. 30 millilitres
1 gill (¼ pt.)	app. 145 millilitres
½ pt.	app. 285 millilitres
1 pt.	app. 570 millilitres
1 qt.	app. 1.140 litres

Oven Temperatures

	°Fahrenheit	Gas Mark	°Celsius
Slow	300	2	150
	325	3	170
Moderate	350	4	180
	375	5	190
	400	6	200
Hot	425	7	220
	450	8	230
	475	9	240

Flour as specified in these recipes refers to plain flour unless otherwise described.